EXPLORE THE WORLD

SOCIAL SCIENCE

S0-DZE-777

Mighty
Brave Girls

MICHÈLE DUFRESNE

TABLE OF CONTENTS

PIONEER VALLEY EDUCATIONAL PRESS, INC

COURAGE AND DETERMINATION

There are many different ways to be brave. Sometimes you set out to be brave. Other times you end up being brave not because you wanted to but because you had to. Here are three true stories about amazing girls who inspired many people with their courage and determination.

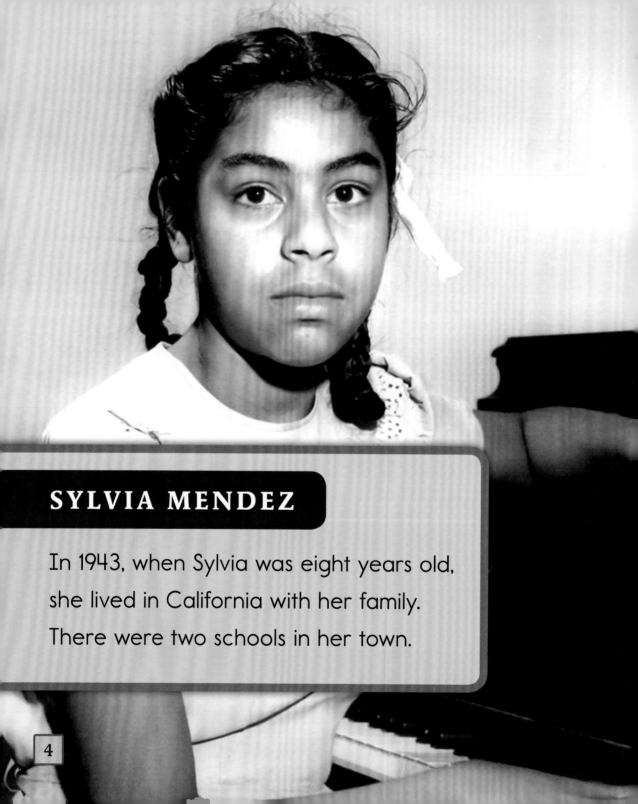

SYLVIA MENDEZ

In 1943, when Sylvia was eight years old, she lived in California with her family. There were two schools in her town.

One school was known as "the Mexican school." It was a two-room shack with very few books or supplies. The other school was only for children with white skin. It was a big, beautiful brick building with a nice playground. Inside, there were lots of books to read.

Sylvia's father felt that she and her brothers should be allowed to go to the nicer school. He believed that they would get a better education there. But the school officials would not admit Sylvia and her brothers because they had brown skin.

Sylvia's father did not believe that this was fair, so he hired a lawyer to take the case to court. The lawyer found other families from different school districts who also wanted their children to go to the better school.

Sylvia's parents

At the **trial**, the judge listened to arguments from both sides and decided that a good public education should be open to all children. Sylvia's family was delighted, but their fight was not over. After the first trial, the whites-only school still refused to let Sylvia in. The school asked for another trial. It was three years before Sylvia and her brothers were allowed to go to the school of their choice.

NO DOGS NEGROES MEXICANS

LONESTAR RESTAURANT A
Dallas, Texas

MORE TO EXPLORE

Through the 1950s, there were some places in the United States that were **SEGREGATED** by race. It wasn't just schools—pools, parks, and even movie theaters had rules about who was and was not allowed to enter. Store windows would often display signs that read, "No dogs, Negroes, or Mexicans allowed."

Going to the new school was not easy for Sylvia. Some of the students called her names and treated her poorly. Sylvia knew her father had worked hard for her to attend the school. She bravely kept going to the school, even when the other children were mean to her.

Sylvia graduated and went to college to become a nurse.

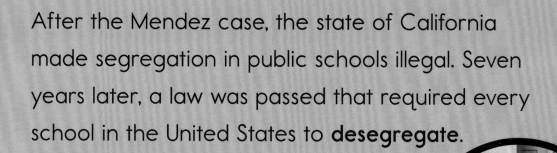

After the Mendez case, the state of California made segregation in public schools illegal. Seven years later, a law was passed that required every school in the United States to **desegregate**.

Some people continued to protest school desegregation even after the law was passed.

In 2010, Sylvia was awarded the Presidential Medal of Freedom.

MALALA YOUSAFZAI

Malala grew up in Pakistan as part of a Muslim family. Her father was a teacher and a builder. He built the school that Malala and her brothers attended.

Malala loved going to school. She loved reading books and learning about the world.

Islam is a religion with more than **ONE BILLION FOLLOWERS**. Followers of the Islamic faith, like Malala and her family, are called Muslims.

MORE TO EXPLORE

When Malala was ten years old, a **violent** group called the Taliban took over the Swat Valley area where she lived. The Taliban believe that females should not leave the house without a male relative. They also believe that girls should not go to school, and they even destroyed many schools in the area. The Pakistani army tried to stop them, and Swat Valley became a dangerous place to live. Many girls stopped going to school, but not Malala.

Malala wrote all about her life under the Taliban's rule on a blog called *Diary of a Pakistani Schoolgirl*. She used a pen name to protect her family.

"Let us pick up our books and our pens. They are our most powerful weapons."

— MALALA YOUSAFZAI

One day, the Taliban fighters stopped Malala's small school bus as she traveled home with her friends. The Taliban fighters shot and wounded Malala. She survived the gunshot and was flown to a hospital in England where she recovered.

Getting shot did not stop Malala from speaking out. When she recovered, she was invited to talk to groups around the world about the right for all children to get an education.

On the day she turned 18, Malala opened a school for teenage girls in Lebanon.

MORE TO EXPLORE

Malala has met with Queen Elizabeth II and **PRESIDENT BARACK OBAMA.**

At 17 years old, Malala was the youngest person to be awarded the Nobel Peace Prize.

15

CLAUDETTE COLVIN

Claudette grew up in Alabama during the 1950s at a time when white people and black people were segregated. There were laws that kept black people from using the same bathroom or water fountain as white people.

When black people rode the city bus, they could only sit in certain seats at the back. Even if all of those seats were taken, a black person could not move to a white person's seat. They would just have to stand. And if a lot of white people got on the bus, the driver would tell the black people to give up their seats.

At the age of 15, Claudette had a frightening experience on a bus. She had taken a seat on her way home from school before the bus filled up. A few stops later, some white people got on the bus, and the driver told Claudette and her friends to give up their seats. Claudette's friends got up to stand at the back of the bus, but Claudette did not. She decided she could not obey this unfair rule anymore. The driver yelled at her and called two police officers to drag her off the bus. They handcuffed her and locked her in a jail cell.

Claudette was **ARRESTED** nine months before Rosa Parks (pictured below) was arrested for not giving up her seat on a bus.

MORE TO EXPLORE

Claudette's mother and their pastor got Claudette out of jail. After that, the news spread quickly that a teenage schoolgirl had been arrested for refusing to **surrender** her bus seat to a white passenger. Claudette was the first person to challenge the law of segregation on buses. Her fearless actions inspired others to join in the fight for equality.

GLOSSARY

desegregate
to allow people of different races or religions to meet with one another

segregated
keeping people of different races or religions separate from one another

surrender
to give up control to someone else

trial
a meeting in a court with a judge

violent
using physical force to cause harm

INDEX